Use a S

by Lucy Long

I like to draw houses.
I use shapes in my art.

2

I like to make a quilt.
I use shapes in my art.

I like to paint pictures.
I use shapes in my art.

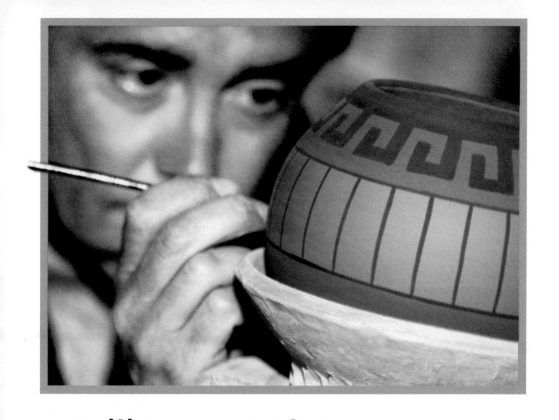

I like to paint pots.
I use shapes in my art.

Can you see the shapes?

Art I Like

Talk to a partner about the book.
Which art do you like best?
What shapes do you see?

Shapes I Draw

Make a picture with shapes. Write
about the shapes you drew.

I drew a _____.

Shapes All Around Us

GR 4 • Benchmark C • Lexile 140

Grade K • Unit 2 Week 2

www.mheonline.com

The **McGraw·Hill** Companies

ISBN-13 978-0-02-119431-5
MHID 0-02-119431-9

99701

EAN

9 780021 194315

K